First Word Book

KINGFISHER

KINGFISHER

Kingfisher Publications Plc
New Penderel House
283-288 High Holborn
London WC1V 7HZ
www.kingfisherpub.com

First published by Kingfisher Publications Plc 2000
First published in paperback 2002
4 6 8 10 9 7 5 3 (hb)

2RD/0303/TIMS/SCH(SCH)/150 MA

2 4 6 8 10 9 7 5 3 1 (pb)

1TR/0302/TIMS/SCH(GR)/150MA

A CIP catalogue record for this book is available from the British Library.

ISBN 0 7534 0441 9 (hb)   ISBN 0 7534 0484 2 (pb)

Printed in China

Editor: Camilla Reid
Senior Designer: Sarah Goodwin
Illustrator: Mandy Stanley
DTP Co-ordinator: Nicky Studdart
Production: Caroline Jackson
Educational Consultant: Jeni Riley

Contents

Suggestions for parents   4

What's in the bedroom?   6

Things we see in the kitchen   8

It's bathtime!   10

Getting dressed   12

Point to these parts of your body   14

What food do you like to eat?   16

Look around the garden   18

Let's go to the park!   20

There's lots to do at school   22

The supermarket is a busy place   24

We are going to a party   26

Who are these people?   28

Things that go   30

Come for a day on the farm!   32

Where do these animals live?   34

Having fun at the seaside   36

What's the weather like?   38

What sounds do these make?   40

Can you name these shapes?   42

All sorts of opposites   44

What's your favourite colour?   46

Word list   48

Suggestions for parents

Sharing a favourite book with your child is the ideal way of helping him or her learn to read. This colourful, appealing first word book will act as an invaluable prompt for looking at, discussing and labelling everyday objects, and it will establish the skills needed for confident reading.

Very young children will enjoy browsing through the book, pointing out objects they recognise. Encourage them to show you what they know about each picture and give them plenty of praise, even if they get things wrong. For toddlers, the book will help them to learn about both spoken words and written words and the connections between the two. This is important in the very earliest stages of learning to read.

When reading this book with your child, we suggest you progress through the steps listed opposite. Try to create a relaxed, non-pressurized atmosphere and allow your child to work at his or her own pace. Above all, remember that for learning to be valuable, it should also be fun!

4

1. Point to the objects on each page. Say each label then ask the child to repeat them. After several readings, he or she will start to say the names unprompted.

2. Match the spoken word to the written label next to the picture. Encourage your child to run a finger along the written label (this develops the understanding that a spoken word has a written equivalent).

3. Select a picture label and ask your child to find the same word in the list that runs along the bottom of the page. This teaches the child to recognise the shape of the word, an essential pre-reading skill. Initially, the child may just realise that the text looks the same, but eventually you can point out the shape and distinctive features of the individual letters.

4. Encourage your child to identify words by the common initial sound/letter, and then to realise that a letter (or group of letters) represents a sound within a word, e.g. the <u>ch</u> of <u>ch</u>ick.

Enjoy your reading!

Jeni Riley

Jeni Riley M.A., Ph.D., Head of Primary Education,
Institute of Education, University of London

What's in the bedroom?

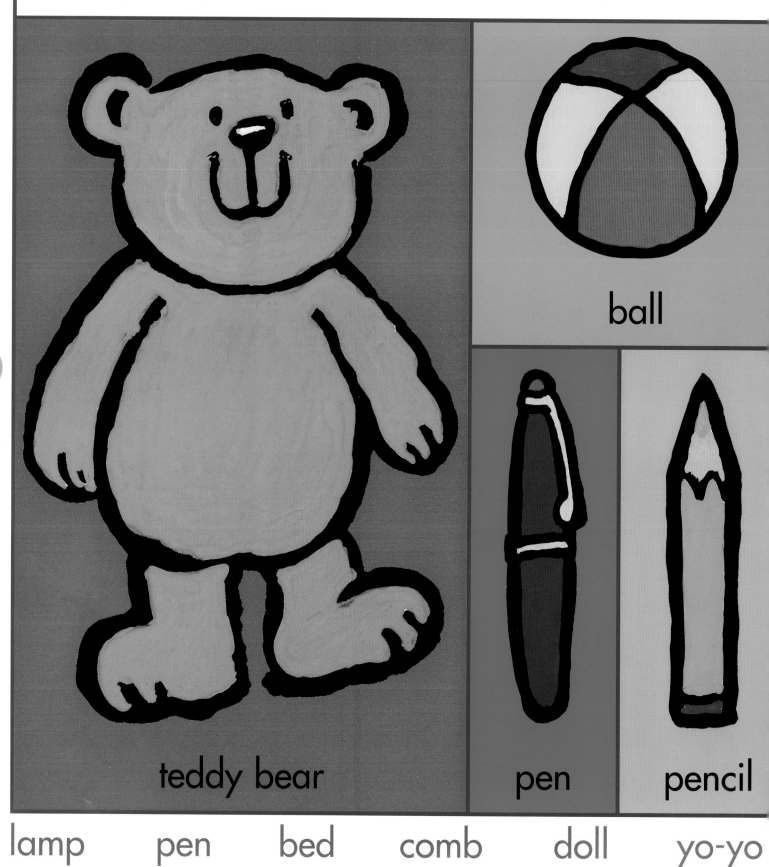

teddy bear

ball

pen

pencil

lamp   pen   bed   comb   doll   yo-yo

6

bed

lamp

yo-yo

rug

comb

kite

book

doll

kite   ball   pencil   rug   book   teddy bear

Things we see in the kitchen

fork

knife

spoon

iron

plate

bowl

spoon   mop   bib   jar   mat   pan

jar

mop

bib

pan

mat

cup

cup　　fork　　bowl　　iron　　plate　　knife

It's bathtime!

bath

duck

sponge

towel

toothbrush   sink   potty   door   bath   soap

sink

door

mirror

potty

toothpaste

soap

toothbrush

toothpaste mirror duck towel sponge

Getting dressed

T-shirt

skirt

jeans

trainers

socks

jumper   shoes   cap   T-shirt   skirt   gloves

coat

gloves

jumper

shoes

belt

cap

scarf

trainers   scarf   belt   jeans   socks   coat

Point to these parts of your body

nose

toe

back

chin

14

ear   back   nose   hand   knee   foot

ear

hair

foot

arm

hand

eye

leg

knee

hair   eye   arm   leg   chin   toe

What food do you like to eat?

pineapple

bread

banana

orange

egg

pie

lolly   strawberry   carrot   bread   cheese   pie

ham

carrot

cheese

apple

strawberry

lolly

banana   pineapple   egg   orange   ham   apple

Look around the garden

butterfly

slug

rake

ant

ladybird

worm   cobweb   frog   ant   gate   butterfly

18

bird

gate

cobweb

leaf

nest

frog

worm

slug   ladybird   rake   nest   bird   leaf

Let's go to the park!

pushchair

dog

pond

sandpit

flower   tricycle   rollerblades   see-saw   pond

flower

swing

rollerblades

tricycle

tree

slide

see-saw

swing   tree   sandpit   dog   pushchair   slide

There's lots to do at school

table

teacher

paints

paintbrush

bricks   rucksack   blackboard   chair   table

drawers

bricks

scissors

rucksack

chair

blackboard

paints scissors paintbrush teacher drawers

The supermarket is a busy place

milk

jam

trolley

assistant

box   purse   tin   juice   till   vegetables

vegetables

bag

box

tin

till

juice

purse

money

money   bag   assistant   milk   trolley   jam

We are going to a party

cake

candle

balloon

present

sandwich

party-blower

bow   candle   sweets   hat   present   straw

jelly

bow

sweets

hat

straw

cake   balloon   sandwich   party-blower   jelly

Who are these people?

woman

girl

man

boy

baby

girl   clown   nurse   boy   dancer   spy

vet

chef

dancer

clown

spy

dentist

nurse

chef   baby   dentist   man   vet   woman

Things that go

ship

rocket

car

aeroplane

bus

motorbike   train   bicycle   rocket   lorry   car

bicycle

boat

hot-air balloon

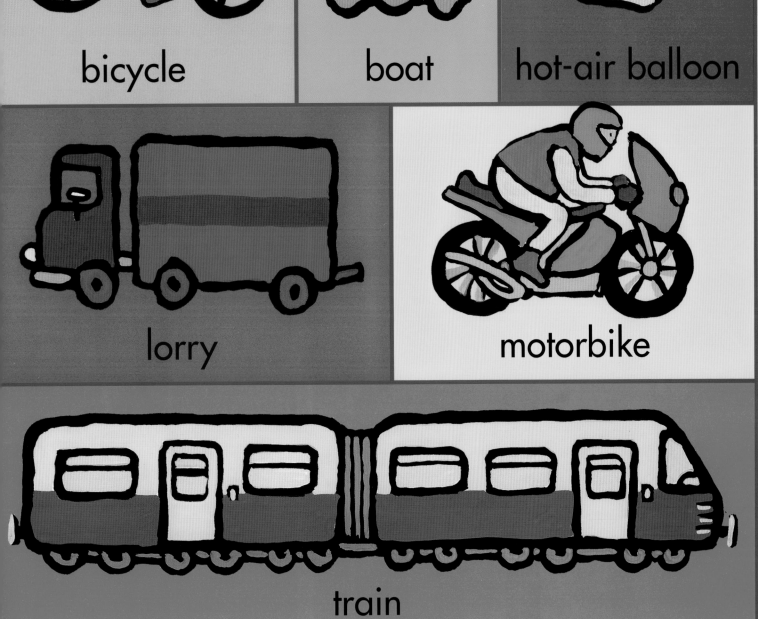

lorry

motorbike

train

boat   ship   hot-air balloon   bus   aeroplane

Come for a day on the farm!

tractor

goat

barn

pig

bull

cat   sheep   house   farmer   chick   bull

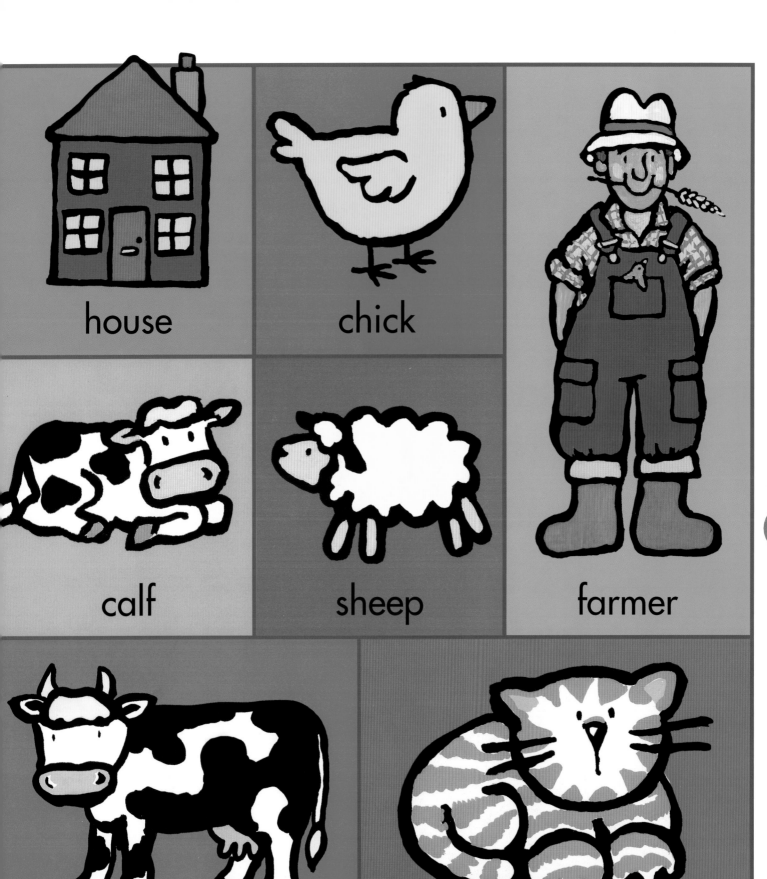

house

chick

calf

sheep

farmer

cow

cat

goat   calf   pig   barn   cow   tractor

Where do these animals live?

tiger

wolf

swan

deer

bear   parrot   deer   tiger   seal   monkey

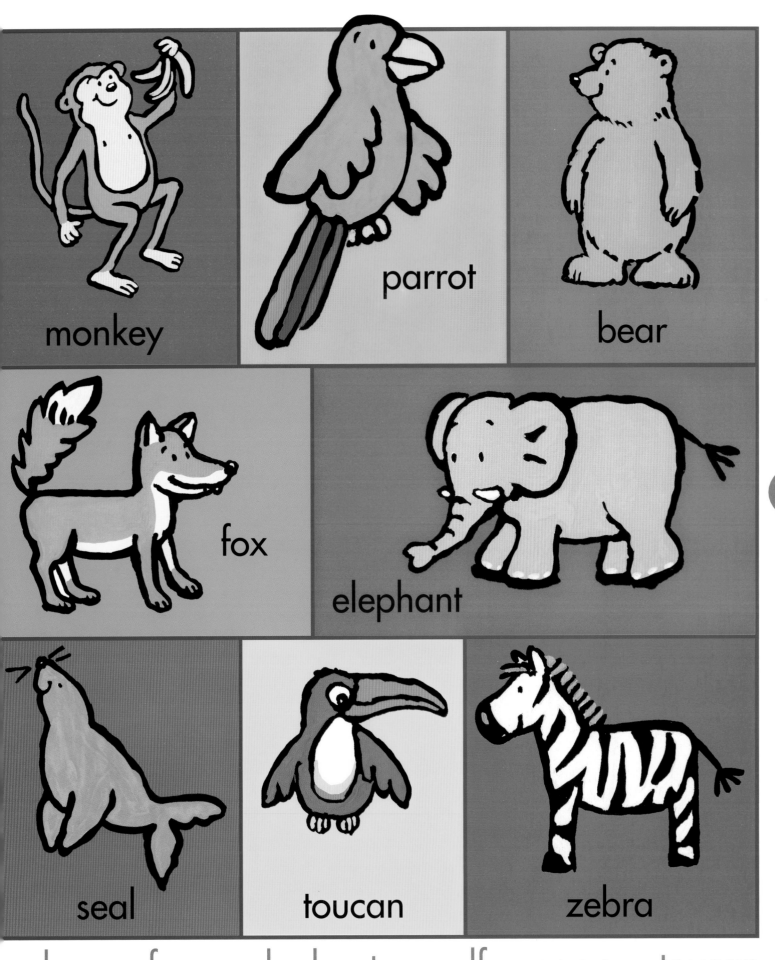

monkey

parrot

bear

fox

elephant

seal

toucan

zebra

zebra   fox   elephant   wolf   swan   toucan

Having fun at the seaside

starfish

sea

fish

flip-flops

yacht

36

sea   bucket   crab   shell   fish   sandcastle

eel

sandcastle

crab

spade

net

bucket

shell

net   spade   yacht   flip-flops   eel   starfish

What's the weather like?

sun

hail

lightning

fog

rain

storm   wind   ice   hail   cloud   sun

ice

snow

moon

cloud

wind

storm

rain   moon   lightning   snow   fog

What sounds do these make?

bang bang

drum

horse

clip clop

bee

buzz buzz

ding dong

bell

woof woof

dog

mouse   snake   lamb   bee   trumpet   lion

ring ring

telephone

snake

hiss hiss

squeak squeak

mouse

baa baa

lamb

roar roar

lion

41

toot toot

trumpet

owl

twit twoo

bell owl horse drum telephone dog

Can you name these shapes?

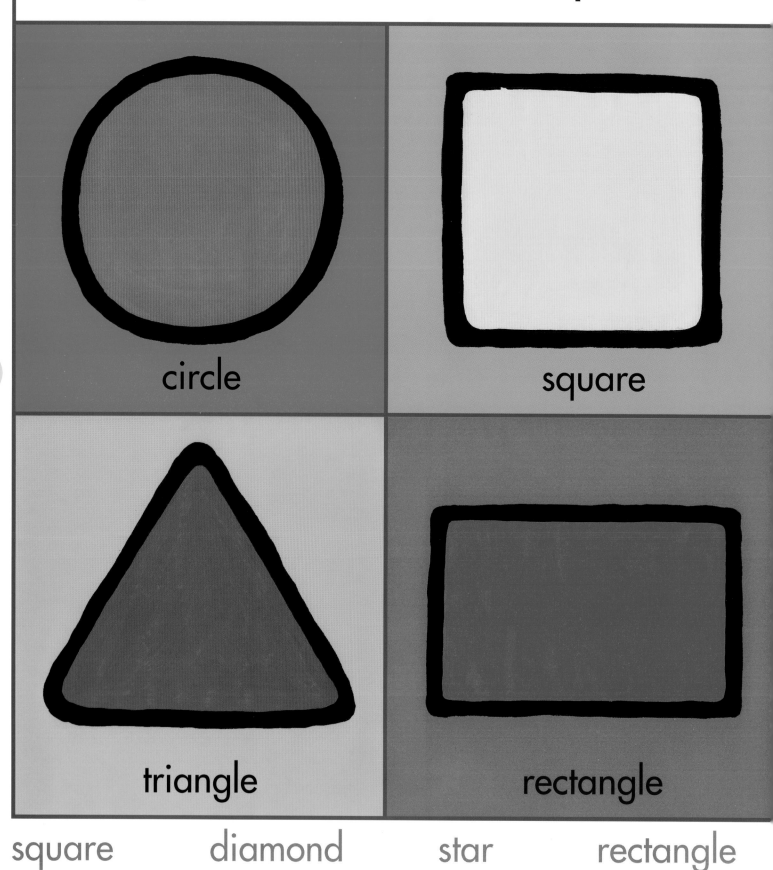

circle

square

triangle

rectangle

square   diamond   star   rectangle

42

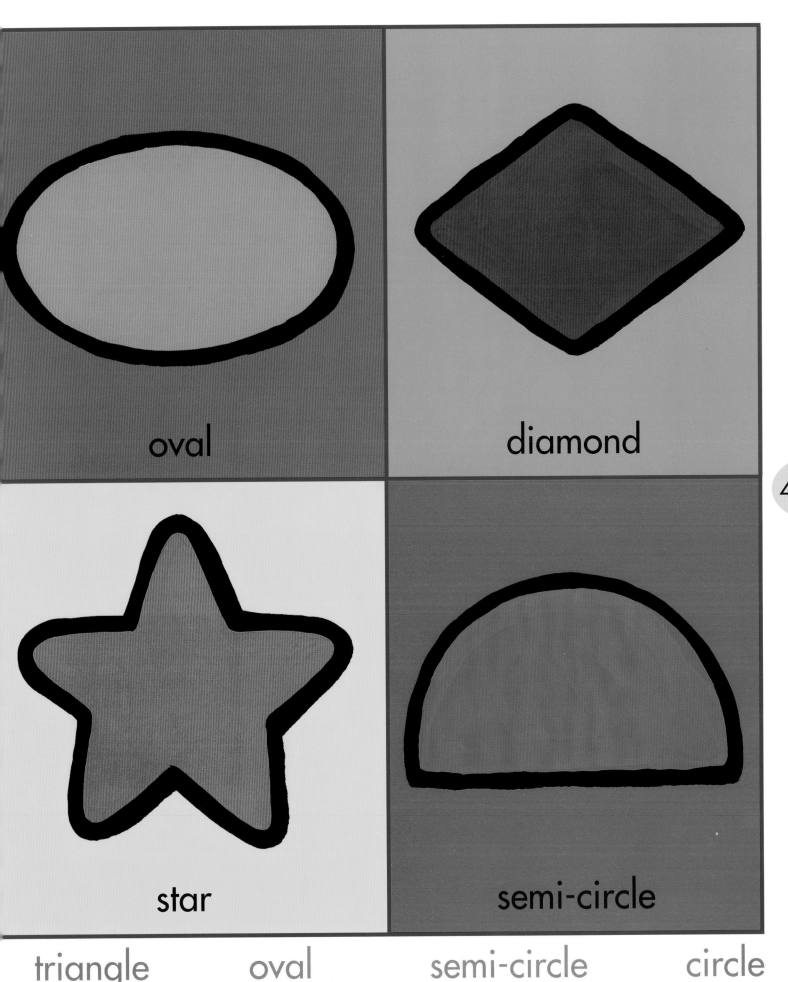

oval

diamond

star

semi-circle

triangle   oval   semi-circle   circle

All sorts of opposites

fat

thin

old

young

slow

fast

big   young   up   short   fast   thin

up

down

tall

short

big

small

slow   small   tall   down   old   fat

What's your favourite colour?

black

yellow

green

blue

white   brown   pink   yellow   orange

grey

purple

red

brown

pink

white

orange

grey   black   green   purple   red   blue

Word list

A
aeroplane 30
ant 18
apple 17
arm 15
assistant 24

B
baby 28
back 14
bag 25
ball 6
balloon 26
banana 16
barn 32
bath 10
bear 35
bed 7
bee 40
bell 40
belt 13
bib 9
bicycle 31
big 45
bird 19
black 46
blackboard 23
blue 46
boat 31
book 7
bow 27
bowl 8
box 25
boy 28
bread 16
bricks 23
brown 47
bucket 37
bull 32
bus 30
butterfly 18

C
cake 26
calf 33
candle 26
cap 13
car 30
carrot 17
cat 33
chair 23
cheese 17
chef 29
chick 33
chin 14
circle 42
cloud 39

clown 29
coat 13
cobweb 19
comb 7
cow 33
crab 37
cup 9

D
dancer 29
deer 34
dentist 29
diamond 43
dog 20, 40
doll 7
door 11
down 45
drawers 23
drum 40
duck 10

E
ear 15
eel 37
egg 16
elephant 35
eye 15

F
farmer 33
fast 44
fat 44
fish 36
flip-flops 36
flower 21
fog 38
foot 15
fork 8
fox 35
frog 19

G
gate 19
girl 28
gloves 13
goat 32
green 46
grey 47

H
hail 38
hair 15
ham 17
hand 15
hat 27
horse 40
hot-air balloon 31

house 33

I
ice 39
iron 8

J
jam 24
jar 9
jeans 12
jelly 27
juice 25
jumper 13

K
kite 7
knee 15
knife 8

L
ladybird 18
lamb 41
lamp 7
leaf 19
leg 15
lightning 38
lion 41
lolly 17
lorry 31

M
man 28
mat 9
milk 24
mirror 11
money 25
monkey 35
moon 39
mop 9
motorbike 31
mouse 41

N
nest 19
net 37
nose 14
nurse 29

O
old 44
orange 16, 47
oval 43
owl 41

P
paintbrush 22
paints 22

pan 9
parrot 35
party-blower 26
pen 6
pencil 6
pie 16
pig 32
pineapple 16
pink 47
plate 8
pond 20
potty 11
present 26
purple 47
purse 25
pushchair 20

R
rain 38
rake 18
rectangle 42
red 47
rocket 30
rollerblades 21
rucksack 23
rug 7

S
sandcastle 37
sandpit 20
sandwich 26
scarf 13
scissors 23
sea 36
seal 35
see-saw 21
semi-circle 43
sheep 33
shell 37
ship 30
shoes 13
short 45
sink 11
skirt 12
slide 21
slow 44
slug 18
small 45
snake 41
snow 39
soap 11
socks 12
spade 37
sponge 10
spoon 8
spy 29
square 42

star 43
starfish 36
storm 39
straw 27
strawberry 17
sun 38
swan 34
sweets 27
swing 21

T
table 22
tall 45
teacher 22
teddy bear 6
telephone 41
thin 44
tiger 34
till 25
tin 25
toe 14
toothbrush 11
toothpaste 11
toucan 35
towel 10
tractor 32
train 31
trainers 12
tree 21
triangle 42
tricycle 21
trolley 24
trumpet 41
T-shirt 12

U
up 45

V
vegetables 25
vet 29

W
white 47
wind 39
wolf 34
woman 28
worm 19

Y
yacht 36
yellow 46
young 44
yo-yo 7

Z
zebra 35